RAYANNA HARDIE

Chatter & Strategy to Level Up in Real Estate

simple conversation, simple strategy for new agents and not so new agents to bring solid success

Copyright © 2024 by Rayanna Hardie

All rights reserved. No part of this publication may be reproduced, stored or transmitted in any form or by any means, electronic, mechanical, photocopying, recording, scanning, or otherwise without written permission from the publisher. It is illegal to copy this book, post it to a website, or distribute it by any other means without permission.

Rayanna Hardie asserts the moral right to be identified as the author of this work.

Rayanna Hardie has no responsibility for the persistence or accuracy of URLs for external or third-party Internet Websites referred to in this publication and does not guarantee that any content on such Websites is, or will remain, accurate or appropriate.

Designations used by companies to distinguish their products are often claimed as trademarks. All brand names and product names used in this book and on its cover are trade names, service marks, trademarks and registered trademarks of their respective owners. The publishers and the book are not associated with any product or vendor mentioned in this book. None of the companies referenced within the book have endorsed the book.

First edition

This book was professionally typeset on Reedsy.
Find out more at reedsy.com

Contents

Chapter 1	1
INTRODUCTION	2
ALL ABOUT YOU	4
QUALIFY, QUALIFY, QUALIFY	8
SELLER'S	12
BUYER'S	17
OBJECTION HANDLING	21
CLOSING	23
CLIENT RETENTION FILE	25
FINDING CLIENTS	27
There is enough complication in Real Estate that I believe...	29

Chapter 1

WELCOME IN…
THIS GATHERING OF INFORMATION IS GEARED TOWARDS NEW REALTORS AND REALTORS THAT WOULD LIKE TO BECOME MORE ESTABLISHED AND LEVEL UP TO WHAT THEY SEE OTHERS AROUND THEM DOING… BEING SUCCESSFUL! WITH SOME SYSTEMS IN PLACE IT IS ATTAINABLE..DO IT EVERY TIME, AND THEN REPEAT…
COME ON IN, TAKE YOUR OFF SHOES, PUT YOUR FEET UP… again…welcome in…

"Establishing trust is better than any sales technique."…. Mike Puglia

INTRODUCTION

When I started Real Estate.. It was 25 years ago...I decided to become a realtor on a wing and a prayer! And definitely only on a dime... My Mom bought me a couple new suits and a pair of shoes and my sister let me use her turquoise aged minivan (I say this with such a smile on my face) I had business cards printed on cheap paper... and I was just really ready to make some money because well.. I didn't have any.

Thinking back and realizing at the time the situation that was looming before me was daunting...

I joined a brokerage..went to the tuesday morning sales meetings, and quickly realized I didn't know what to do.…

This is a howto, an accumulation, ideas, gleaned over coffee, overheard from conversations and well lessons that people were willing to tell me, share with me, and some I paid for in how to classes. We could call this confessions of an aged realtor but I am still active today and these systems, techniques, and processes still work today. If you have a program you are following this will complement it, if you have no systems in place this will give you some. The best thing about what I will tell you is that you can choose to follow these things because they work. Some take practice, some will make you feel the fear (but

INTRODUCTION

you do it anyway), some will land with a resounding bang and you will say..THAT WAS EASY!.. Always an afterthought but isn't that the way of it. Once we find out something works we feel obligated to do it again.

" Excellence is not a skill, it is an attitude." ….Ralph Martson

ALL ABOUT YOU

(BECAUSE IT IS REALLY ALL ABOUT THEM!)

I find sometimes we feel we have to dress a certain way, drive a certain car...but really? We can just raise ourselves to a standard of being clean, dress as business casual as you can and make sure our car is the best it can be ..especially clean and running with the gas tank filled up. Sometimes the finer things come later but a standard raised of- in order (clean, repaired) works really well with humanity in general.

I worried when I only had the old van but won some clients because I said ..I know you don't want to leave your children with a babysitter.. I have a minivan so let's load everyone up and get going! They decided right then and there I was their realtor because of that. Years later I drove a high end luxury car and was concerned in case someone thought I made too much money, and clients told me they were happy that their realtor was successful! Point being our thoughts about ourselves are just that, thoughts about ourselves that need to be settled and handled .. just like any objection.

I was worried when I thought I looked like a brand new realtor and how would they have any confidence in me...

The first client I had actually did ask me how long I had been a realtor and I looked at my watch and said " oh about 5 or 6 minutes now..!"

ALL ABOUT YOU

Then I said but here is the deal… I just got a really good education… if there is something I don't know I have a great team I can call on but I have all the newest methods on the books..so I looked 'em square in the eye.. And said "You ready to get going?" …I actually practiced this stuff in front of a mirror. Anything to build confidence.

1. Write out what success is to you, know why you signed up to be a 100% commission based salesperson! That right there provides substance to the soul. Being a realtor shows lots of promise and lots of reward (always in the future!) So knowing your own commitment level can take you right to where you want to go. Make a plan of what you will do everyday.. Book your days off first. (when you first start sometimes you do have to work some of those)

You can take a course or read a book about filling your day timer or digital calendar and priorities but it must be done. Knowing when you will work and when you will have time for other commitments..even sleep is important to you, your survival and your family and friends. One of the biggest parts of being a realtor is personal integrity. It bleeds into every area of our lives and business. A line in the sand is all it takes to decide how you will spend your time, your money, what kind of thoughts you will have..so really that integrity word ends up determining the level of peace we go home with…

In your calendar block off times when you will have an appointment even if you presently don't have any. Your goal is to fill them with income creating activity and ultimately appointments.

1. Real Estate is not an I got " lucky " type of business. Standing

around the office and exchanging stories or hiding at home or at the coffee shop.. Does not the bills pay nor make the savings account grow. You must have a plan to be in front of people and talking about real estate on a regular basis. Real Estate really is a numbers game.. In sales talk it is said if you talk to about 25 people about Real Estate that are actually interested in Real Estate there will be 5 people that will do a deal over the next year and 1-2 people now..so you need to be face to face with people on a regular basis to do a deal, to find buyers, to find sellers. There are lots of marketing techniques from open houses, to writing ads, sending letters.. Until you have developed a client base that will give referrals you need to find and decide on some income producing marketing techniques and learn them.

1. SHOW UP and LISTEN UP… for everything..sales meetings, events. Mostly with a great attitude, be happy..acting happy even when we arent can make us happy.

I listen to podcasts, talks, other successful realtors..even now. I don't, do nor do I agree with everything I hear but it created in me a confidence to try a new thing in an area where I am struggling. I have been in the industry for a while and I must stay updated but mostly my systems with people and closing and handling objections never changes. A system I put in place over the years. I do the same thing with every buyer, and every seller. I follow the same listing conversation and process and I show houses the same way every time.

1. So in taking care of yourself, educating yourself, deciding how

to act, talk, and live and breath and assessing yourself after the job is done will ultimately take precious care of your buyers and sellers… because really you aren't here to sell or buy your own house but you are a realtor to create an income for you and your family to live and move and breath.

While we do always want to present our best that we have in clothes, shoes…it really doesn't matter in the long run how new your shoes are, it matters what you believe you are in those shoes..and how you are represented in them.

" I am not a product of my circumstances. I am a product of my decisions." …Stephen Covey

QUALIFY, QUALIFY, QUALIFY

Before anything else…

The old saying "buyers are liars' really is not true..If there is a buyer who is lying it is because we the Real Estate Agent have not equipped them. Either we don't know the questions to ask or we are too afraid to ask them or another one is we ask offensively (which is a whole other book !)

Whether you get a buyer from a sign call, an internet call, a website, a referral, an open house, at the local coffee shop,… wherever, it does not matter. I deal with them the same way. And I rate them according to a letter or a number or a star system. You can use any one of those. I use a letter system because I have used it since I started and I do the same thing all the time. Whatever way I get them, in talking on the phone, or in person I kick into wanting knowledge of them to qualify whether I am able to work with them. (when you are new it is okay to work with people whether they qualify or not, just so you learn. You still spend the time to qualify but you decide at that time if you have time to work with a C or D client) When I was new I made the decision to work with whatever came across my plate so that I gained knowledge. Even lots of those lower qualification people came back to me later when they could complete because they already saw me as their Real Estate Agent. They had already seen me work hard and felt a sense of "I was their agent"

So the qualifying questions?..all opened ended starting with the most important one
1. WHEN?

- Are you thinking of buying
- Are you thinking of selling

Always wait for the answer... learn to hold your tongue
Right there is your biggest answer in qualifying
**30-60 days?!...
That is an A or an A+ client. Typically it means their motivation level is high and finances are probably in order or they are motivated to get them in order
**2-3 months..
That could be a B client. Typically might have a financial hiccup or just a timing issue. Sometimes they are an A in disguise! Because they just don't know how fast or slow the market is..maybe they don't make decisions quickly.

**6 months..
That could be a C client..might not be able to purchase or sell until finances or personal life is more in order. When you aren't busy they are great clients to take on and build rapport with.
** when I find a good deal
Okay here is typically a D client. I cut my real estate teeth on D clients. I ran all over the place for them and learned so many lessons. My education was extensive!! They truly want to find a good deal, and if they dont they wont sell or buy. Simple. All of us should work with

D clients as long as we are also working with the other letters. Some of those D clients did find their "good deal" or they suddenly increased their motivation because of life and I was the one they called. You always want to be the one they are going to call.

All of this to say it is okay to work with them all, just so long as you know what type of client will be more income producing and which client will provide an education to you at your expense ;)

So then you move into the rest of those questions.
 WHO?...who are the buyers? Will both people on title be at the appointment?(always make sure all parties are present)

WHAT? Neighborhood? Style?, schools important? Etc

WHERE? City, Surrounding towns? Close to city center, suburbs? Etc

HOW? Do you have pre approval, how much?, down payment? Gifted? These are for before appointment..don't be afraid to ask. No down payment , mortgage broker said no..they don't get in the car...unless you need to work with C and D clients... sometimes when you listen between the lines you can hear of something that may be able to be fixed.

WHY? This one can be asked when you are with them but it is important to find out your clients story as much as possible so you can know them and start providing a safe place for them to purchase or sell. That safe place is with you.
 Real Estate or so "they" say is always a good investment...only a good investment if you are in a position to hold. For how long? As long as it takes.. I always tell my first time buyers when they ask if they will

lose money.. Don't put yourself in a position to HAVE to sell.. So while you are living and breathing carve out a way of life that you can count on. Save while you are spending, no credit card debt, make a plan. Try not to get divorced then you could be forced to sell when the market is down. A home will increase in value over the years..it is solid. If the market falls just hold and wait for recovery and the increase in the market. History proves it will come back again.

" I never lose. I either win or learn." ...Nelson Mandela

SELLER'S

It doesn't matter what business you go into.. You will find a system. A business needs a system. A system is a collection of procedures or ideas that produce results..simply put it is a way that puts in place the outcome for a desired effect. It creates success when you have a good system.

When working with sellers all you need is a good one!

I do the same thing all the time.

1. Go to the door and knock

..on the way up the sidewalk I take in as much as I can. I notice deficiencies, good and bad curb appeal, bushes that need trimming, flower beds that need wedding, grading? Shingles?

Broken concrete? Rusty mailbox, dirty threshold? I also look at the neighbors lawn and care of their yard. I have suggested my sellers mow the neighbors lawn or shovel their snow before we list and as we progress.

When they answer the door I am friendly and warm. It seems often the sellers really don't know what to do with you so this is where you order the appointment.

" It is so nice to finally meet you folks! Instead of us looking through the home right now (they often will suggest it), lets go to the kitchen

SELLER'S

table and we can discuss our time together (if they have to clear off the kitchen table, let them, even help them) Once everyone is situated this is the time you will build rapport. Dont tell your own stories... be so interested in theirs they want to know yours but only give small warm answers. It truly is all about them right now..and who do people like to talk about?.. Themselves , yes.

Determine an amount of time for this. Use pointed questions within their story to find out why they want to sell...their motivation level, how much they think their house is worth? They usually say they don't know that is why you are here but my answer to that is. Oh ! I have the price but I want to know how you value your home what you think of it with just your best guess. Always call people to action by saying you've got them, it's okay but what is important to me as your real estate agent is knowing where their mind and heart is on the matter. This lets you how much work you do or don't have in settling on a price for their home in the present market.

I do address their price... if it is low I tell them so and justify it with what has sold and what they have in their home. I sayBecause you have cared for this home I think we can ask a bit more.. If they are too high I say as your agent I wish I could sell it for 600,000 even if it is worth around 400,000. I want you to be happy with me but because that price has no determination in this present market I will show you how we can determine fair market value based on what is fact in this market (which happens to be sold because that is fact. Not what other sellers are asking because until it is sold that is fantasy). I assure them they will be part of determining sale price based on information we seek together. We look at CMA, I print out hi-lite sheets and hand out highlighters we mark them up together using those properties that are similar in comparison to theirs. I dont ever give a price ..this amount and not a penny more! I explain I do not use a crystal ball but base on fact and market alone. This has instilled confidence in sellers to work along side me that we are partners in this and I am not the salesperson coming in trying to get a quick sale. I try to create an environment and relationship where they feel valued. I guess though that I really do value them.

I ask what they are prepared to do in the home besides the list we will determine together during the walk thru ie: kitchen counters totally cleared off, bathrooms clean and cleared, nice towels etc etc etc.

I ask what upgrades have been done and explain most of the time lots of those make the home more saleable not necessarily more valuable. I proceed very carefully during this part to determine what they think already and how we can achieve a good outcome for them together. We talk scenarios left right and center. It is my goal that the sellers feel they are working along side me to accomplish this. This result will be directly related to my building rapport with them in the beginning and being in control of the situation gently and confidently. At the kitchen table is a real opportunity for you to present yourself as kind, a listener, educated, respectful and warm warm warm to them. It is a time to be NICE. Others always want to be with people that are nice.

When we do the walk thru, I ask the hard questions…will you make the beds every morning? Will the dirty underwear be put away for showings? Of course these questions are not in every house but it doesnt matter however hard they are you must ask them…

I do give suggestions pertinent to that home when we sit down. Make sure toilet seats are down, nice towels hanging, beds made, clothes picked. Please dust and vacuum. Toys must be put away. I also tell them buyers now are trying to buy a dream. They want turn key and they want to see that they could live their dream here! Even though when they move in they live like we all do…I have helped my clients over the years with small things especially seniors or disabled people that are compromised physically somehow. My last client had wrong day marked down for pictures so when I arrived we vacuumed and swept and picked up, loaded dishwasher ,wiped counters, shone taps, mirrors together!! No need to say more.

    I show them sold properties (proper market evaluation) and we determine price together. I always tell them when they are too high. It is very important I am clear about price. I do tell them I will list even if price is aggressive (if they are pushing) but we will need to reduce the price when they are tired of showings with no offer. So I have set them up for price reduction instead of giving an inflated price to buy the listing. That rapport in the beginning works wonders. I always tell my clients when I take phone calls/texts. And response time. I tell them no response from me means I am with people just like I dont answer my phone when I am with them, but I make sure to return text/call as soon as I am free. I always try to tell people ahead of time how I will respond during the process then there are no disappointed expectations.

    I fully believe the reason Sellers/Buyers become really good clients is because of equipping them for future scenarios, how I responded in the past...the information I give that is pertinent to them about them about their deal. I tell them of things that can happen ,what I do to prevent that but if it does happen we see what needs to be done at the time. I work on deflating situations before they inflate!!

    I instruct my sellers on the whole situation....determining price, showings, other agents not showing up for showing (ugh), forgetting to leave a card, leaving window open, no feedback etc etc.

    I leave with the listing if they are an A or B seller. I go for signature of contract with a later start date and handle any objections right then and there. I ask is there any reason you would not sign this now and then settle those reasons to signature.. Being kind, and diligent for them. It is my job to have them excited to work with me...

So again..

Step 1...knock on door

Step 2...go to kitchen table

Step3...build rapport, be nice, be diligent..be sincere

Step4...find out how you can help them, find the reason

...are you competing with other agents. I explain that they are only able to provide the same info that I can. I would be excited to work with you and I sense you believe I am able to do the job so my suggestion is lets get this signed now and let me start the ball rolling. Give those agents numbers to me and I will cancel the appointment for you so you dont need to deal with it at all.

Now this is a hard close but it will work, lots of the time. If rapport and trust and personal interest has been provided with care from the start, no reason to not take the listing then. Now you continue to act in a way they are confident in you from start to finish. A person of your word, on time, and knowledgeable. If you don't know, say so and get back to them with the answer.

" Success seems to be connected with action. Successful people keep moving. They make mistakes but they don't quit." Conrad Hilton

BUYER'S

Let me tell you one thing about working with Buyers! They are fun... In Real Estate...buyers and sellers want to know they have someone that is working for them. They want to know how you will work for them. So when I am with buyers I tell them.

"Just so you know I am not one of those agents that will show you 3 or 5 houses and then expect you to pick one!" I tell them I love showing houses and why shouldn't you see what is in your price range and location and style so you can make a really good decision. I would like you to see enough product out of what is available where you say to me..."this is a good house, good price... I think this may be it! I tell them there is a good chance based on others that they may find it today but it make take a couple times going out before you they want to make a move on a place. I also tell them it doesn't matter what I do and don't like..I am not paying for it so I will keep my thoughts to myself unless I see an issue for resale or high cost (which I will point out). I am not here to get a quick sale overnight but I am here to do such a good job they will refer to me! You have to let people know you want referrals. This is why your system must be strong. Write out your process..at what times you do this or that or introduce this or that.

I don't ever "sell" a house. I always walk up to a house with my buyers and point out something negative... because it lets them know I am not trying to sell the house but just provide opportunity to show it. This also encourages them to point out stuff to me so they feel like they are discovering things also. It is a time for me to handle an objection with them and prepare them for things to come. If they are in a trust position with me they will absorb this information of any problems equipping themselves to make a decision knowing that no property is perfect. The fewer surprises at inspection time the better it is. I often agree that this(whatever is an objection) is a concern and if they decided to write on it an inspector would help us determine if the issue at hand was workable or walkable.

I always tell them to go through the house with me following..I don't need to point out that a bathroom is a bathroom..any questions and I am right there. If they are nervous at first I tell them what we should or should not touch in a house and the expected routine of me following ,me responding to their questions.. Us leaving the house in the same order as when we entered. Shoes off, no taps running, doors locked and lights off when we leave. They get the hang of it really quickly and often remind me to leave a card and did I lock the doors? I find clients really respond to the process when they are informed and there are no secrets. I tell them if they do see a house they would like please tell me because if they like that means someone else will like it also! There are only ever a few good houses in a certain price range. Sometimes one ..so lets go find it. I also say if we walk in and you just dont like it ..tell me and lets leave ..no use to waste time.

Working with buyers is the same as any other part of Real Estate. I always leave time at the start of showing for a new client to go over paperwork and sign what we need..yes right in the car. We always go to a coffee drive through to start and grab coffee, breakfast sandwiches, donuts... on me. People love to receive. I always join them and we enjo it together. I chat! I ask about their kids, their job, how long they have been married, what they do for a living...again there is a rendition of Who What When Where Why... they think I am interested..because I am! It is so easy to make showing houses fun. I tell them on the phone..HEY! I will pick you guys up, we will stop for coffe and go and have some fun looking at homes.. They always are excited.

But no politics or religion is best...always about them.

I dont show houses out of their parameters or price range. I inform of that in the beginning. It saves me from saying no to "Oh can we go see that house? I know we cant afford it but we would love to see it!" no we cant because I already handled that objection in the beginning. I stay in touch with buyers as properties come and like to find them before they do so they know I am working for them. Again due diligence is a beautiful thing. A great marker towards success.

I want buyers by my side. I dont like when they travel in their cars because I want them working out the viewing in my car with me and looking at the next property we are going to. We are a team.. A team travels to the game on the bus together. The one that gets a ride from someone else feels on the outskirts.

My biggest goal in dealing with my business is to do just that. Be in control of my business systems and processes and that includes making my buyers and sellers feel like they are cared for and protected in the midst of a huge decision and being worked for.

Every client from start to finish. A complete process. I write bullet points and check them off. We discuss looking for a property and what that looks like, writing an offer and all parts of it, inspection, conditions, waivers, lawyers, title insurance, to Possession day. The best client is an informed client...no surprises. How I will negotiate for them..when I won't negotiate for them...when there is no negotiation left, the line in the sand, and when I will go full throttle and what happens when we accomplish everything and when we don't.

" If you're not making mistakes, then you're not doing anything." …John Wooden

OBJECTION HANDLING

How do we as sales people handle objections? You know... I often say, I dont sell houses. What I really do is handle objections...

1. This house is falling apart
2. How much is your commission
3. I cant buy this
4. They are taking advantage
5. That is too much money
6. They are trying to hide defects
7. They left all the lights on
8. They let the cat out
9. We cant list now we are interviewing other agents
10. We want to go home and crunch numbers
11. Our parents want to see the place first

... You get the idea

How you handle an objection..any objection is you handle it before it happens. Don't ever react in a situation to an objection. I sit with buyers and sellers before go time and I inform them of things that could arise. When said things (see above) show up my clients may address it with me but they ask..is this one of those times?..yes you we talked about such and such and they say okay. I still handle it as we go but they don't carry the offense of the objection with, they instead seem equipped to deal with it..with me of course. So again... Deal with objections before they happen by equipping clients with the answers and possibilities. A good example is " can we renegotiate the price after inspection? " If they dont ask I bring it up. I always say no it is so you know what you are buying. Any added negotiation would only be pertinent to an extreme issue and having said that if it was so extreme maybe they wouldn't want the home. So if any negotiation needs to happen they have the correct perspective.

When I started Real Estate so many years ago I was told by someone that I respected to produce a list of as many objections as I could think of and to find an objection handling technique or 2 for each one. Practice them, know them. Then when you are with people you are equipped and dont present as not knowing what to do. When you run into a new objection(and you will) add it to your list, then add the solution..then carry on.

" The way to get started is to quit talking and begin doing." ... Walt Disney

CLOSING

Handling Objections and Closing in Real Estate are the meat and potatoes of the industry. Fine tuning these skills is what will equip you for success down through the years.

Closing works beautifully when you have a plan. No plan is like planning to fail...we have all heard that. If you have been up front and informative with your clients and created a semblance of urgency your closing experience can be seamless. Buyers always ask "how much should I offer?" I always respond with.. You tell me. I will tell you if you are too low or too high. I don't want you to pay a penny more than you will have to... and we proceed from there. By this point they should know I am on their side. I also show them what others have paid in the same market. If we are in a sellers market that is fast I equip them from the start for an over list offer... if we are in a buyers market I bring their offer down knowing I have skills to feel out and assess a situation... all things I was not born with but have learned throughout my career. I try to ask questions that I know the answers to. In closing I have no trouble getting the offer or contract signed with a successful (mostly) outcome because of the relationship I have developed with my clients since start date. Closing isis beautiful when people are equipped with the knowledge they need to make an informed decision. The day I meet them I start to close…one of the first things I leave with is "Hey?!…just so you know no question is too silly, or wrong..make a list of them..I probably know the answer but if I dont I will find out for you, promptly."The next thing I do amidst all contracts is go for a verbal commitment."..Every single time.

I ask outright…did I answer any questions you had? Do you feel I am equipped to help you find a house? I even throw in " do you think I am fun?" anyway..in 25 years after the initial meeting no one has refused me.. "I say this is how I make my living so I need to know will you use me as your realtor?" I shut my mouth and maintain eye contact and wait for the answer…. When I get a yes I hold my hand out and shake theirs. I tell them I believe people are good to their word. And I am going to work hard. Because I want to do such a good job they will want to trust me with their family and friends.

CLIENT RETENTION FILE

Everyone always needs a way to keep track of their clients...I remember when i started out I thought I would never forget a client name and certainly never their new address! Well... it happened. Ha!..there is a simple paper... i used to hand draw it..now you can do it in your phone, on your laptop in a program...whatever you like , the biggest thing is to just do it, the one you like the best.

Name _____ Qualify_A,B,C,D?
   Bank/Broker____
   Wants, location,price,schools etc___
   WHEN?
   WHAT?
   WHERE?
   WHY?
   HOW?
   Completion____ Gift___ Keys____
   Something like this for every client..every time

Anything like the above will do until you find a system that you want to use, maybe this works for you... then you transfer them into a permanent client list.

Keep in touch with your clients a few times a year. Email them or for a real treat send a hello and market update by snail mail. Call them to ask how they are, how is the new home, do they know of anyone interested in buying or selling real estate. Always ask for referrals! When a client or future client or acquaintance gives a referral always acknowledge it with a thank you card or email and anything else you have decided to do for referrals.

Keeping in touch with people of course keeps your name and face in their minds. This can be worked on as you go. A card at Christmas and some sort of something....a calendar, a notepad..bigger is not always better.

You can start on a budget and make your contact with people sincere and genuine..it is really about the relationship and not the doo dad, pen, or keychain.

FINDING CLIENTS

There are many ways to find clients...

*Running ads to make the phone ring (using when, where,..when being most important to qualify!) The phone is to make the appointment always...all talk is about them. Be cheerful, open, inquiring about them. Be nice!

* Open Houses for other agents in your office. Put out signs (borrow them from someone in your office until you can afford your own). Always make sure house has good curb appeal or people won't come in. You probably won't sell that house so know everything that is for sale in the area. If people that are looking are not working with an agent (ask them)...then when they say this house doesn't have a white kitchen like we wanted, your'e response can be ," oh yes I understand.. You know I am finished this open house in 30 min, why don't we meet here and I know of couple houses in this price range and one of them has a white kitchen ...why dont we just get in and have some fun looking at them? Then you build rapport constantly and that is small example of an opportunity to acquire a client. Even neighbors will come to open house. Is there a chance they want to sell themselves?

*When you start Real Estate send a letter(yes it is still a great idea to post a letter) and email to everyone you know saying you are loving the business of Real Estate.

Send some market news about prices, days on market..etc and a call to action.. "If you or anyone you know is interested in buying a home or selling their home then give a call or an email" Don't be the best kept secret!

These are just a few ideas..the thing about Real Estate whatever you do be diligent and systematic. When you find an idea that produces, then work it with excellence into your system. It will become effortless.

" You are never too old to set another goal or dream a new dream."... C.S. Lewis

There is enough complication in Real Estate that I believe we need something simple and these ideas ARE just that. Plus they bring with them a sense of like I suggested some pages before…THAT WAS EASY!

Always deal with them the same way..
    *Quality and in doing so you are not working for nothing
    *Build rapport..always right up front, be integral
Work with all clients the same way.. Build and practice a system.
    *Inform all clients of existing market and how they will be expected to respond in price possession…all things contractual.
    *Make your clients feel valuable now and they will stay with you for years, they won't do Real Estate without you.
    *Have a great objection handling file…Build it!
    *Close all clients…always ask for the signature, ask for the offer… ALWAYS ask for commitment to use you as their agent.

Welcome into Real Estate..an opportunity to create a real business that can care and provide for you and your family, that can care and provide expertise to your clients and their family…through the years..One step at a time, One process at a time…One paycheck at a time.. Then watch the increase come. This book is just like a small minute..really just the suggestions made here with diligence can take you up and out of whatever state you are in..just not knowing what to do next, feeling confused, whatever it is..it can be better with small systems put into place..one step at a time and repeat!

I wish for you…systems to make your career calculated, where you know the outcome….

Real Estate has a lot to offer..I wish you the very best of it!!

RESOURCES

https://solofire.com/blog/60-motivational-sales-quotes-to-fire-up-your-sales-reps/

www.ingramcontent.com/pod-product-compliance
Lightning Source LLC
Chambersburg PA
CBHW072056230526
45479CB00010B/1108